MING WARRIORS

VS.

MUSKETEERS

45th Parallel Press

Published in the United States of America by Cherry Lake Publishing
Ann Arbor, Michigan
www.cherrylakepublishing.com

Reading Adviser: Marla Conn, MS, Ed., Literacy specialist, Read-Ability, Inc.
Book Designer: Melinda Millward

Photo Credits: © Aisyaqilumaranas/Shutterstock.com, back cover, 6, 10; © Marcin Szymczak/Shutterstock.com, cover, 5; © LifetimeStoc/Shutterstock.com, cover, 5, 16; © Sunwand24/Shutterstock.com, 9; © Unholy Vault Designs/Shutterstock.com, 12; ©Pictorial Press Ltd / Alamy Stock Photo, 15; © GraphicsRF/Shutterstock.com, 19, 20; ©Pictures From History / AGB / age footstock, 19; © vectortatu/Shutterstock.com, 20; © Yongsky/Dreamstime.com, 21; © toiletroom/Shutterstock.com, 23; © Voropaev Vasiliy/Shutterstock.com, 24; © HelloRF Zcool/Shutterstock.com, 25; © bergamont/Shutterstock.com, 25; © Ke Wang/Shutterstock.com, 27; © Photo12/Pierre Pitrou/ The Image Works, 29

Graphic Element Credits: © studiostoks/Shutterstock.com, back cover, multiple interior pages; © infostocker/Shutterstock.com, back cover, multiple interior pages; © mxbfilms/Shutterstock.com, front cover; © MF production/Shutterstock.com, front cover, multiple interior pages; © AldanNi/Shutterstock.com, front cover, multiple interior pages; © Andrii Symonenko/Shutterstock.com, front cover, multiple interior pages; © acidmit/Shutterstock.com, front cover, multiple interior pages; © manop/Shutterstock.com, multiple interior pages; © Lina Kalina/Shutterstock.com, multiple interior pages; © mejorana/Shutterstock.com, multiple interior pages; © NoraVector/Shutterstock.com, multiple interior pages; © Smirnov Viacheslav/Shutterstock.com, multiple interior pages; © Piotr Urakau/Shutterstock.com, multiple interior pages; © IMOGI graphics/Shutterstock.com, multiple interior pages; © jirawat phueksriphan/Shutterstock.com, multiple interior pages

45th Parallel Press is an imprint of Cherry Lake Publishing.

Library of Congress Cataloging-in-Publication Data

Names: Loh-Hagan, Virginia, author.
Title: Ming warriors vs. musketeers / by Virginia Loh-Hagan.
Other titles: Ming warriors versus musketeers
Description: [Ann Arbor : Cherry Lake Publishing, 2019] | Series: Battle royale : lethal warriors |
   Audience: Grades: 4-6. | Includes bibliographical references and index.
Identifiers: LCCN 2019003643| ISBN 9781534147706 (hardcover) | ISBN 9781534150560 (pbk.) |
   ISBN 9781534149137 (pdf) | ISBN 9781534151994 (hosted ebook)
Subjects: LCSH: China—History—Ming dynasty, 1368-1644—Juvenile literature. | Soldiers—China—Juvenile
   literature. | France—History—Louis XIII, 1610-1643—Juvenile literature. | France. Mousquetaires du roi—
   Juvenile literature. | Soldiers—France—Juvenile literature. | Imaginary wars and battles—Juvenile literature.
Classification: LCC DS753 .L64 2019 | DDC 944/.032—dc23

Printed in the United States of America
Corporate Graphics

About the Author

Dr. Virginia Loh-Hagan is an author, university professor, former classroom teacher, and curriculum designer. She's Chinese American. So, she's rooting for the Ming Warriors. She lives in San Diego with her very tall husband and very naughty dogs. To learn more about her, visit www.virginialoh.com.

Table of Contents

Introduction

Imagine a battle between Ming Warriors and musketeers. Who would win? Who would lose?

Enter the world of *Battle Royale: Lethal **Warriors***! Warriors are fighters. This is a fight to the death! The last team standing is the **victor**! Victors are winners. They get to live.

Opponents are fighters who compete against each other. They challenge each other. They fight with everything they've got. They use weapons. They use their special skills. They use their powers.

They're not fighting for prizes. They're not fighting for honor. They're not fighting for their countries. They're fighting for their lives. Victory is their only option.

Let the games begin!

In real life, nobody really wins in a war.

MING WARRIORS

The first Ming emperor was Zhu Yuanzhang.
He was born a poor farmer.

The Ming **dynasty** ruled ancient China. Dynasty means ruling family. Ming rulers were called **emperors**. Emperors needed protection. The first Ming emperor created a Ming army. Ming Warriors guarded emperors. If the emperor died in war, any living warriors would be killed. Warriors fought to win or die.

Most Ming Warriors **inherited** their positions. Inherited means to get as an heir. Sons became Ming Warriors after their fathers died. If a warrior died, families sent another warrior.

People could become Ming Warriors. They had to pass military **exams**. Exams are tests. Ming Warriors were tested on many things. But the most important was horse **archery**. Archers shoot bows and arrows while on a horse.

Ming Warriors had a system. They were very ordered. They were grouped. Emperors had guards. Guards had about 5,600 men. Each guard was divided into **battalions**. Battalions are troops ready for battle. Battalions had about 1,120 men. Each battalion had 10 **companies**. Companies are military groups. Each company had about 112 men. Each company had 2 **platoons**. Platoons were teams with special skills or jobs. There were about 56 men in each platoon. Each platoon had five **squads**. Squads are teams. Each squad had about 12 men.

Southern soldiers were good land fighters. Northern soldiers were good sea fighters. Each naval battalion had about 50 ships. They set up fences. They set up towers. They set up forts.

Most Ming Warriors couldn't read or write.

Ming Warriors used many weapons. They used fire **lances**. Lances are long poles. Warriors used spears. They used **pikes**. Pikes are long poles with blades. Warriors used bows and flaming arrows. They used shields. They used **sabers**. Sabers are curved swords. Ming Warriors used long guns. They used gunpowder weapons. They shot rockets.

They wore a coat of iron plates. The coat went to their knees. It didn't cover arms and legs. It protected their chests. But it let them move.

Ming Warriors took care of themselves. They made their own food. They had their own military farms. They took turns training. They took turns working. This was so they wouldn't get tired and quit.

FUN FACTS ABOUT MING WARRIORS

- The Ming dynasty ruled for 276 years. Ming means "brightness." The first Ming emperor chose this name. He felt the last ruling dynasty was a dark period. He wanted his rule to be bright. The Ming dynasty was a time of growth.

- Zheng He was born around 1371. He led 7 navy trips. He explored the "western oceans." He led a large fleet of ships. His ships carried treasure. They carried horses and troops. They carried fresh water. They impressed foreign countries. They showed the power of the Ming Empire.

- Ming emperors helped build the Great Wall of China. They used stone. Troops guarded the work. They took turns. They lived in watchtowers with their families.

- The capital of the Ming dynasty was Beijing. It was called the Purple Forbidden City. Purple refers to the North Star. Over 24 rulers lived there. The Forbidden City is surrounded by a wall. The wall is 26 feet (8 meters) high. It has a 20-foot-deep (6-m) moat. Moats are ditches filled with water.

MUSKETEERS

There were many plans to kill the king during the time of the musketeers.

Musketeers used **muskets**. That's how they got their name. Muskets are long guns. They hit through armor. They were invented in the 16th century. The most famous musketeers were the King's Musketeers. They served the king of France and his family. They served the king when he was outside of his home. They were his royal guard. They were his bodyguards. They were his secret service. They were his special forces.

They wore uniforms. They wore black leather gloves and boots. They wore leather hats with feathers. They wore light coats. Their coats had the king's symbol. This meant they belonged to the king.

A team of musketeers also guarded the **cardinal**. Cardinals are senior leaders of the Catholic Church. They're the "princes of the church." They advised the king. They were second in charge.

Musketeers were highly respected. Most musketeers were **nobles**. Nobles are people with royal blood. They're connected to the French royal class. Not all of them were rich. Becoming musketeers helped them get richer.

Musketeers had a lot of training. They had "**esprit de corps**." Esprit de corps means team spirit. They fought with zest. They fought as **infantry**. Infantry are foot soldiers. Musketeers fought as **cavalry**. Cavalry are soldiers who fight on horses.

In the book, *The Three Musketeers*, the King's Musketeers and the cardinal's musketeers fight.

Musketeers had to be strong to use muskets. Muskets could weigh up to 20 pounds (9 kilograms). They fired big bullets. The bullets were 1 inch (2.5 centimeters) wide. Musketeers needed strength to load and fire. But muskets changed. They became lighter. They became easier to use. **Bayonets** were placed at the end. Bayonets were blades. This turned muskets into swords.

Musketeers had gun power. They had good aim. But they were good swordfighters too. They always had their swords. They also carried **daggers**. Daggers are small knives. Musketeers also used **grenades**. Grenades were small hand bombs. Musketeers were ready to fight at any time.

FUN FACTS ABOUT MUKSKETEERS

- King Louis XIII ruled from 1610 to 1643. He turned France into a leading European power. He founded the king's Musketeers in 1622. He gave muskets to a company of soldiers.

- Alexandre Dumas was a famous French writer. He was inspired by the musketeers. He wrote *The Three Musketeers*. This book is based on real history. But it's fiction. It made the musketeers famous.

- Musketeers inspired a candy bar. The candy bar is covered in chocolate. Inside is nougat. Nougat is made by whipping egg white and adding sugar. From 1932 to 1945, there were 3 flavors. The flavors were chocolate, strawberry, and vanilla. That's why it's called Three Musketeers.

- Flintlocks were invented in France. They were invented in the early 17th century. They were invented by Marin le Bourgeoys. Muskets used flintlocks. Soldiers pulled triggers. A spring action struck the flint. This showered sparks onto gunpowder. The lit powder fired the bullet.

CHOOSE YOUR BATTLEGROUND

Ming Warriors and musketeers are fierce fighters. They're both trained to fight in battle. They both use the same weapons. Ming Warriors are better with gunpowder and long poles. Musketeers are better with muskets and horses. They also have better armor. Both groups are good with swords. They're well-matched. But they have different ways of fighting. So, choose your battleground carefully!

Battleground #1: Sea

• Ming Warriors are strong sailors. They explore faraway lands. They have a strong navy. They defend their coasts. They battle **pirates**. Pirates are sea robbers.

• Musketeers don't fight many sea battles. But the French went to sea. They explored. They had **colonies**. Colonies are areas owned by another country.

Ming Warriors who went to sea were called "ocean imps."

Battleground #2: Land

• Ming Warriors live in China. China covers a lot of land. It has a lot of enemies. Ming Warriors are used to fighting on land. They've fought against different groups.

• Musketeers follow the king or cardinal. Most kings and cardinals stay close to home. Leaving is too risky. Musketeers mostly stay on land.

Battleground #3: Mountains

• Ming Warriors have fought on mountains. China has 7 of the world's 12 tallest mountain peaks. Over 65 percent of China is **rugged**. Rugged means rocky and uneven.

• Musketeers live in France. France is mostly flat. It has gently rolling hills in the north and west. It has mountains in the south.

ARMED AND DANGEROUS: WEAPONS

Ming Warriors: The Chinese invented gunpowder. Ming Warriors used cannons. Cannons are guns. They shoot out firepower. They had used thousands of cannons. They used cannons in naval battles as well. They put cannons on their warships. The Chinese used metal to build their cannons.

Musketeers: Musketeers were good swordsmen. They always had rapiers by their side. Rapiers are thin swords. They have sharp points. They're 3 to 4 feet (0.9 to 1 m) long. This was so rapiers could be used for slashing. Musketeers didn't sharpen the bottom part. This was so rapiers could block hits. Rapier handles were shaped like cups. They could be used to punch and smash.

FIGHT ON!

The battle begins! Ming Warriors and musketeers have arrived. The musketeers are protecting their king's honor. The two groups meet in an open field. They form battle lines. They agree to meet in the middle.

Move 1:

Ming Warriors prepare to do the "Mandarin Duck." Mandarin means Chinese. This is a military **formation**. Formations are organized groupings. Ming Warriors get into groups of 12 men. Each group has a leader. The leader is in the first row. The second row is 2 men with shields. The third row is 2 men with short lances. The fourth and fifth rows each have 2 men with long lances. The sixth row is 2 men with **forked** lances. Forked is V-shaped. These lances have 2 sharp tips. A final man stands in the back and carries food and supplies.

Ming Warriors could be hired to do a job.

Move 2:

Musketeers start to line up. They load up their muskets. They get into a line. Soldiers with pikes line up. They're ahead of the musketeers. They're on their horses. Their pikes are 18 feet (5.5 m) long. Musketeers need time to reload their guns. These soldiers protect them.

Move 3:

Ming archers on horses are in the back. A separate group of Ming Warriors with guns move forward. They cover the Ming Warriors in formation. Each leader yells at men to march. The men march together in formation. They march toward their enemies. They bend their heads. They hide their bodies behind their shields.

The number of musketeers in service was 150 to 300 men.

LIFE SOURCE: FOOD FOR BATTLE

Ming Warriors: Rice is a main food item for Chinese people. So, Ming Warriors ate rice. Rice can last a long time. It's easy to move. It's easy to cook. It's easy to swallow. It gives energy. It tastes good. It can be eaten with anything. Ming Warriors ate one bowl of rice per day. They had to ration food. Ration means to make things last.

Musketeers: Stories say baguettes were invented for French soldiers. They were carried in soldiers' pants. Baguettes are long sticks of bread. They're thin. They have crisp crusts. They bake quickly. They can be easily carried. They're tied to backpacks. Pieces can be torn off. They can be eaten while moving. France has a lot of bakeries. Bakeries are places that make and sell bread. An average French person eats half a baguette a day.

Move 4:

Musketeers stay. They force the Ming Warriors to come to them. The soldiers lower their pikes. Musketeers aim and shoot. Their bullets fire away. They hit some Ming Warriors.

Move 5:

Ming Warriors with guns fire back. Archers shoot arrows. They were waiting for the musketeers to take the first shot. Ming Warriors in formation move forward. They move more quickly. They don't look back. There are so many of them. If they lose men, there are more men to replace them.

Move 6:

Musketeers stop shooting. Muskets are only good for long distances. Ming Warriors are too close. Musketeers take out their swords. They cut. They slash. They try to break the Ming Warriors' formation.

Ming emperors had a standing
army and a navy fleet.

AND THE VICTOR IS . . .

What are their next moves?
Who do you think would win?

Ming Warriors could win if:

- They get rid of the king and cardinal. Musketeers only serve their leader. Without the king or cardinal, musketeers wouldn't get paid.
- They keep their numbers big. There are more Ming Warriors than musketeers.

Musketeers could win if:

- They hired Ming Warriors for a job. Ming Warriors were often hired to do work. Work includes guarding. If they're busy working, then they can't fight.
- They plan surprise attacks. Ming Warriors are good at planning war. They plan strategies.

Musketeers were disbanded in 1816.
The French ran out of money.

Ming Warriors: Top Champion

Qi Jiguang lived from 1528 to 1588. He was a Ming Warrior. He was a general and national hero. He fought against Japanese pirates. He grew the naval fleet. He defended China's southern coast. He fought in over 80 battles. He fought for over 10 years. He worked on the Great Wall of China. He made repairs. He guarded the borders. He built watchtowers. He kept the peace. He achieved many things. But he was a teacher at heart. He recruited miners and farmers. He trained them to be strong soldiers. He trained the Ming Warriors. He created many fighting moves. He created different formations. He also taught martial arts. He wrote 2 books about warfare and training. He wrote many poems. He wrote, "Pretty is not practical. And the practical is not pretty." Practical means real actions. Jiguang was a great military leader. He did what needed to be done.

Musketeers: Top Champion

Marie Joseph Paul Yves Roche Gilbert du Motier was the Marquis de Lafayette. Marquis is a title for a nobleman. Lafayette was born in 1757. He was born in France. He was born into a rich family. He became a musketeer. He was inspired by the American colonists. He liked the idea of fighting for independence. He sailed to the United States. He fought in the American Revolution. He was a major general. He served for free. He was shot in the leg at the Battle of Brandywine. He became good friends with George Washington. (He named his son Georges Washington de Lafayette.) He got France to support the Americans. He helped Americans win the war. He returned to France. He helped organize trade agreements between America and France. He led the national guard. He was called the Hero of Two Worlds. He got sick. He died in 1834.

Consider This!

THINK ABOUT IT!

- How are the Ming Warriors and musketeers alike? How are they different? Are they more alike or different? Why do you think so?
- If the Ming Warriors and musketeers lived at the same time, do you think they would've fought each other? If they did, who would win? Why do you think so?
- Would you rather be a Ming Warrior or a musketeer? Explain your thinking.
- What was the role of women in the world of the Ming Warriors? What was the role of women in the world of the musketeers?
- Why don't we have musketeers in modern armies? How has warfare changed?

LEARN MORE!

- Adams, Simon. *Eyewitness Soldier*. New York, NY: DK Publishing, 2009.
- Cotterell, Arthur. *Ancient*. New York, NY: DK Publishing, 2005.
- Raatma, Lucia. *The Science of Soldiers*. Mankato, MN: Compass Point Books, 2012.
- Tsiang, Sarah, and Martha Newbigging (illust.). *Warriors and Wailers: One Hundred Ancient Chinese Jobs You Might Have Relished or Reviled*. Toronto: Annick Press, 2012.

GLOSSARY

archery (AHR-chur-ee) activity involving the shooting of bows and arrows
battalions (buh-TAL-yuhnz) troops ready for battle
bayonets (BAY-uh-nets) stabbing blades placed at the end of long guns
cardinal (KAHR-duh-nuhl) a senior leader of the Catholic Church
cavalry (KAV-uhl-ree) soldiers who fight on horseback
colonies (KAH-luh-neez) areas owned by another country
companies (KUHM-puh-neez) military groups
daggers (DAG-urz) small knives
dynasty (DYE-nuh-stee) a ruling family
emperors (EM-pur-urz) rulers of an empire
esprit de corps (es-PREE duh KOR) a feeling of pride and loyalty shared by the members of a group
exams (ig-ZAMZ) tests
forked (FORKD) V-shaped
formation (for-MAY-shuhn) a formal arrangement used in military strategies

grenades (gruh-NAYDZ) small hand bombs
infantry (IN-fuhn-tree) soldiers marching or fighting on foot
inherited (in-HER-it-ed) received as an heir at the death of the previous holder
lances (LANS-iz) long poles
Mandarin (MAN-duh-rin) Chinese
muskets (MUHS-kits) long guns
nobles (NOH-buhlz) people belonging to a hereditary class with high social status
opponents (uh-POH-nuhnts) groups who compete against each other
pikes (PIKES) long poles with blades
pirates (PYE-rits) robbers at sea
platoons (pluh-TOONZ) teams with special skills or jobs
rugged (RUHG-id) rocky and uneven
sabers (SAY-burz) curved swords
squads (SKWAHDZ) teams
victor (VIK-tur) the winner
warriors (WOR-ee-urz) fighters

INDEX